# ReCreate Your *Love*

A Guide To Create True Unconditional Love For Yourself, Your Spouse, And Others.

## KARI VAZQUEZ

Thank You God! To my amazing Mom, Dad, Children, Grandson, and awesome Husband, Carlos!

Thank You All For Your Love & Support!

Copyright © 2019 Kari Vazquez
All rights reserved.

This book or any portion thereof may not be reproduced or used in any manner whatsoever without the express written permission of the author, except for the use of brief quotations in a book review.

First paperback edition January 2020

Edited by Kate Allyson
Cover Design by Rob Williams

Paperback ISBN 978-1-7341457-0-0
Ebook ISBN 978-1-7341457-1-7

Published by Kari Vazquez
https://www.passion4visions.com

# Table of Contents

Introduction ............................................................................. 1

1 Forgiveness ........................................................................ 5

2 Unconditional Love ......................................................... 41

3 Communication ............................................................... 75

4 Self-Control ..................................................................... 93

5 Reflect & Project ........................................................... 111

6 Believe ............................................................................ 155

7 Take Action ................................................................... 175

*Hello Dear Friend,*

If you have been struggling in your relationship, having a hard time truly loving who you are with, or your life in general; this guide will help you overcome these challenges. Learning to love again takes time and, more importantly, effort on your part. If you are tired of the cycle you have been living, stuck on the same path going around in circles of love hurt; come take my hand and let me guide you through this new path to ReCreate Your Love.

My name is Kari and I am a Relationship Coach. Thank you for entrusting me with helping you ReCreate Your Love! I'm going to be upfront and honest with you from the beginning: this journey will be hard but totally worth it. I have come out of this part of my journey and I am able to love on a level I never thought possible. My prayer for you is that this guide will take you to a higher place and that you will find that higher level of love you never thought possible.

I was married for 10 years, had 4 kids, then got divorced. Soon after, I married my high school sweetheart, had 1 kid, and almost got divorced. But we reconciled and are now happily married. I went through many years of happy and very sad times. When I almost got divorced again, I was in a really dark place. Getting through that part of my journey has allowed me to be where I am today.

Grab a cup of coffee, tea, or glass of wine. Get your pen and let's dive in.

Now remember, this is a part of your journey. This is not a 3-step process and it's not an overnight project. This is a guide to help you on your journey through love, as you conquer what holds you back from being able to love freely so you can love harder and stronger than ever before. What if you could take the love you know, the parts that aren't working, the parts that are broken, the parts that have broken you, and recreate it, what would that look like?

Finally, I am a Certified Coach. I am not a psychiatrist, psychologist, or therapist. This guide shares my experiences and provides you with relationship tips, and guidance on how to improve your relationships. If you are dealing with mental illness, abuse, or anything that requires professional help, please seek that help. A team has different people in different roles: Coaches, Players, Physical Therapists, Trainers, etc. I play the role of Coach, you are the Player, and make sure you recruit those you need to complete your team.

*Much Love,*

*Kari*

*Love Your Hardest Every Day,
As If It Was Your Last!*

*Kari Vazquez*

# INTRODUCTION

### *Practice Self-Love & Relaxation*

Being in tune with your body is part of self-love. It's like driving your car or caring for your home. With your car you may listen for weird noises and you have routine check-ups, oil changes, etc. With your home, you will keep an eye on things that need to be fixed, maintain the yard, change light bulbs, clean, and maintain things in a certain order.

Our bodies are more important than both of those things. Are you doing daily check-ups, self-tuning, repairing what's broken? Notice if you carry stress in your shoulders, back, neck, or in your head. Do you take deep breaths or shallow breaths? Are you slouched, sitting up straight? Is your back against a chair or a couch? Is your body relaxed or tense?

### *Learn How to Relax*

1. Sit up straight in a chair with your feet flat on the floor. Relax your face, your neck, your shoulders.

2. Let any tension flow down and out your arms, down and out through your legs.

3. *Take deep breaths, and release any tension in your stomach, bottom, and legs (you'd be surprised the tension we hold in our bottoms, especially women).*

*Sit in this relaxed state, feel what it feels like, practice it throughout your day.*

## <u>Gratitude</u>

*Each chapter will have a section for you to practice gratitude. Being mindful of the things we are blessed with and practicing gratitude is so important. It helps us live a healthy and positive life each day. Gratitude is also part of healing. As you go through this book, there will be healing taking place in your heart, mind, body, and soul. There is always something you can be grateful for and this book will help you remember to practice gratitude.*

## <u>Lovework</u>

*Each Chapter will have "Lovework" where you will work through assignments that help you learn how to truly love you, your spouse or partner, and others.*

## <u>Check-Ins</u>

*Each chapter will have a "Check-In" to remind you to check in with how you are feeling after processing and going through Lovework. Getting in the habit of checking in with yourself, your spouse, and your important relationships will help your relationships thrive. I think of this as checking the pulse of your thoughts, feeling, and intentions and checking the pulse of your relationships. You want to be sure there's life and if that pulse is faint, checking in will allow you to identify why and how to improve it.*

## <u>*Time Out - Be Still & Breathe*</u>

*Throughout this book take "Time Out" to be still and breathe. Whether you want to pray, meditate, or take a power nap, just take time to give your mind and your body rest. As you begin to practice this throughout this book, take this practice throughout your life. Taking time out from life's difficulties teaches you how to love yourself and will allow you find more peace and joy in your life. This is a time of surrender, where you leave everything aside and focus on you. Breathe, be grateful, be still, and rest throughout your body.*

- *Be intentional and set your timer for 5 minutes. If you love music, play slow music (no words), sit or lay down, and breathe.*

- *Be focused on your breathing or things you are grateful for.*

- *Be relaxed and mindful of your body from head to toe, how it feels, release any tension, and relax.*

- *Be consistent, listen to your mind and your body. When you need a time out, take it!*

*God has given us the strength, power, and will to decide, to do and to be who He has called us to be. Therefore, there is nothing we cannot do, including forgive. When you feel or think you can't do something, then you won't. Open your mind and your heart to receive freedom from what you've allowed to hold you back.*

# 1

## Forgiveness

*Forgiveness is Key!*

First, let me be clear about what forgiveness is and what it is not. Forgiveness is releasing you from holding on to a wrong or hurtful act against you. Forgiveness is not saying what was done was right in any way and it does not mean you even have to have a relationship with the person who wronged you. But forgiveness frees you to move forward without holding on to extra baggage. If you have been in any type of abusive relationship that the abuser has not acknowledged and sought help for, there should always be forgiveness so you are free, but does not mean reconciliation will occur or even should occur.

I grew up in a two-parent home that had love and problems we hid well. Everyone thought we were a perfect family. The reality is, no family goes untouched from the issues of life. As a child I always struggled to feel like I fit in, I struggled with my relationship with my mom, and I was considered the tough one, out of the siblings, so I tried not to show my feelings. Decades later, I have learned how these challenges and behaviors developed anger and bitterness that showed up in many different ways. I was a rebellious child for a few years, that resulted in many poor decisions on my part. It took me getting to my 30's and reflecting on my life to see how I held so many things in and never truly forgave some of these childhood struggles and decisions I had made.

Looking back now, I have come to understand how things like financial struggles and depression in my family contributed to many of our challenges. Not knowing how to process these things as a child, or the lack of understanding that some of these things existed, brought unnecessary anger that I could have processed better if I did understand. Although I lived in a stable home, with average problems, and a very safe environment, that feeling that I didn't fit in continued into adulthood. I felt very loved by my father and I struggled with my mother. I felt like I was never good enough for her which over time built unforgiveness toward her.

I had friends but always felt like the awkward third wheel and the reality was, it was that same feeling with my family. I spent years feeling ugly and unworthy of true love. So I settled for any kind of love, as I longed for that missing connection. When I was 18 years old and met someone who was willing to "love" me and get me out of my house, I took the offer.

Living with unforgiveness in my heart toward myself for decisions I had made, toward my mom, toward people I felt rejected me, caused many years of unnecessary pain and struggle that I did not have to endure. Unforgiveness led to an I-don't-care attitude, because I thought other people didn't care. This negative mindset was also how I thought I was protecting myself. If I acted like I didn't care, then maybe I could actually not care that I never really processed how I felt growing up.

Unforgiveness is tricky like that, it will have you thinking things that don't really exist or may exist, but are not the way you see them. Unforgiveness I had from my childhood and teen years turned into a habit in my marriage. When you hold on to pain or hurt that has been caused to you, over time it turns into bitterness and you get into a dark place. I stuffed my lack of forgiveness for my perceived pain of rejection. While some of it was real, most of it was lies I told myself and believed. Unforgiveness causes your thoughts and beliefs to be cloudy and unclear. It's like mold, it loves darkness and will grow, if you don't kill it. It eats away at you each time you get hurt, especially in the same type of way.

In my case, I started feeling rejection in my 1st marriage and while I thought I had forgiven my ex-husband, I was only ignoring and stuffing my feelings deep down; as I had done growing up. Growing up, we didn't talk about how we were feeling, we stuffed our feelings deep down until one day they exploded. So when I finally learned what a therapist was and that I could talk to someone about my feelings, I began my journey to understand who I was. Sadly, it wasn't until a few years ago that I came to understand me on a much higher level and I'm not sure that years of therapy contributed much. Instead, my own personal development, research, and lots of questions being asked, is what I believe has allowed me to be where I am today.

Unforgiveness that led to my I-don't-care attitude, then led to me wanting to get out of my parent's house, which then led me right back to the same place, a 10-year marriage full of many uncertainties, more rejection, and pain. While I married a person who meant well and wanted good things, many things were wrong. I hope you have seen the cycle here of unforgiveness, until you find and process forgiveness, you will go in circles and attract the same thing that caused you be feel hurt. Unforgiveness drives us toward deep, dark places in our journey in life. It's like falling in quicksand, except you're the only one that can get yourself out. My anger and unforgiveness led to decades of hurt and pain and I want to help you help yourself, so that you stop living a life of hurt, pain, and unforgiveness. Holding on to things only makes you a prisoner to your hurt and pain.

Forgiveness is easy when you practice it daily and you must do it daily to master it. While it does not come naturally, remember many things don't. Forgiveness is a choice and a decision you make. It's like gratitude, we must practice it daily and create a habit, in order to master it. Forgiveness can be broken down into 3 components: forgiving yourself, your spouse/partner, and others. Each area of this book will start with YOU. When you start with you and take responsibility for what you bring into a relationship, both the good and bad, you can make a conscious decision of what you need to change and what you need to continue doing, or better yet, what you can do on a higher, more amazing level. And when you look at yourself and what God would want from you, then operate on that level, you become unstoppable!

*₃₁ Let all bitterness and wrath and anger and clamor and slander be put away from you, along with all malice. ₃₂ Be kind to one another, tenderhearted, forgiving one another, as God in Christ forgave you.*

*Ephesians 4:31-32*
*English Standard Version (ESV)*

## *Forgive Yourself.*

If you struggle with forgiveness, you probably have not forgiven yourself for times you have failed yourself or others. You will be unable to forgive your spouse or others if you don't forgive yourself. However, before we go there, think of things that you are grateful for about YOU. You can be grateful for anything: your beautiful hair, amazing skin, kindness, strong mind, or career. When we practice gratitude daily, first thing in the morning, before we go to bed, and throughout our days, life comes into focus in a positive way. Gratitude changes our perspective in life. Being grateful for who you are and what you have accomplished in life helps you to love you better. Ultimately, you should be practicing the art of self-love daily, as this will allow you to love others on a higher level. What are you grateful for? Write out your list.

*I am grateful for me because:* _____

_____

_____

_____

_____

_____

Now think about areas in your life that you feel guilt or haven't forgiven yourself. Guilt is usually a good indicator that you have not forgiven yourself. (Some ideas: Are you angry with yourself for not being the best spouse or parent? Have you ever felt bad for not feeling "good enough" or being depressed? Do you need to forgive yourself for not being the best cook or having the cleanest home?)

On next page, write out anything you need to forgive yourself for. You may want to use a separate sheet of paper. You'll find out why later.

*"Nothing in the world is worth having or worth doing unless it means effort, pain, difficulty… I have never in my life envied a human being who led an easy life. I have envied a great many people who led difficult lives and led them well."*

— **Theodore Roosevelt**

## "Forgive It" or "F It" List

_____ (Your Name) I Have Not Forgiven You For…

_____

_____

_____

_____

_____

_____

_____

_____

**BUT TODAY, RIGHT NOW, I FORGIVE YOU FOR IT ALL!**

## *Forgive Yourself!*

Now that you have written out your list of things you have not forgiven yourself for, read it to yourself and forgive yourself.

1. Tell yourself, "I forgive you for it all!"
2. Take responsibility for things you will change and do different, but forgive yourself. If you need to, read each item and tell yourself, "I forgive you!"
3. Identify things that are lies, bring them into the light, and speak truth into your heart, mind, body, and soul. Forgive yourself! Lies you may be telling yourself are that you're not pretty or handsome enough, skinny enough, smart enough, or good enough to live the life you desire. These lies could be the root of your unforgiveness. Because I did not feel good enough as a child, I thought I was not good enough as a wife, and this lie caused me to try and be perfect so I'd be considered good enough. I would try to keep things clean and when it got messy, I felt like a failure.
4. Now cut or rip out the "Forgive It or F It List" page. Put this page aside for now. This step of ripping this page out or cutting it out symbolizes you removing unforgiveness from your life. As you rip it out, say, "F It!" Or pick whatever brings you freedom.
5. Go back and read the things you were grateful for. Can you add more? If so, add more things or people you are grateful for. Convert guilt or unforgiveness you've had to gratitude and write those down.

# Check-In

**How do you feel right now?**

_____

_____

_____

_____

_____

**Is there anything you feel you haven't let go of?**

_____

_____

_____

_____

*Be sure to take more time if needed to process anything you may still be holding on to & practice forgiveness!*

## *Forgive Your Spouse!*

Now that you've worked through forgiving yourself, let's move on to your spouse or partner. However, before you start thinking of all the hurt and disappointments that have caused you to blame or resent your partner, *clear your mind*. First, think about what you are grateful for in them. You may be grateful for the way they care for your kids, for their hard work, for provision, for kind words, their amazing smile, the way they make you smile or laugh, or a gentle touch each day. If you do not have a partner, write down what you will be grateful for in a partner. Take this space to write what you would be grateful to have in a partner, things you would love. Starting with the good and ending with the good will help you keep your mind clear. Write your list here.

***I am grateful for my spouse/partner because:* _____**

_____

_____

_____

_____

_____

Despite feeling grateful, there are times that we build up a wall around people and things that have hurt us. As the hurts and disappointments grow, the wall gets higher and the space in that prison cell you created with unforgiveness gets smaller. The walls must come down and you are the only one that can free yourself. You cannot fully live your life behind walls. Remember, this is a choice and a decision that you can make to be free.

Think about all the issues, anger, disappointments...whatever comes to mind that relates to your spouse or partner that you have not truly forgiven them for. On the next page, write out anything they've done to hurt you or disappoint you that you have not forgiven them for. The purpose of this Lovework is to identify anything that comes to mind that you have not forgiven or that you're still holding on to in a negative manner, that you will forgive and let go of. If you can have closure and lump moments into a category, feel free. The point is not to bring up past hurts and the details, but rather to bring up the hurts you continue to bring up or think about because you have not let go.

## "Forgive It" or "F It" List

_____(Spouse/Partner/Ex) I Have Not Forgiven You For…

_____

_____

_____

_____

_____

_____

_____

_____

**BUT TODAY, RIGHT NOW, I FORGIVE YOU FOR IT ALL!**
Do this even if they have not asked for your forgiveness!

## *Forgive Them!*

Almost Done. Now that you have written out your list of things you have not forgiven your partner for, read it to yourself and forgive them.

1. Tell yourself, "I forgive (their name) for it all!"

2. Take responsibility for hurts you may have caused, change that behavior in you, and forgive them for their part. If you need to, read each item and tell yourself, "I forgive them!"

3. Identify things that are lies, bring them into the light, and speak truth into your heart, mind, body, and soul. Forgive Them! Lies you may be telling yourself about them are that they don't truly love you, that they're not trustworthy, or that they will never change.

4. Now cut or rip out the "Forgive It or F It List" page. Put this page aside. This step of ripping this page out or cutting it out symbolizes you removing unforgiveness from your life. As you rip it out, say, "F It!" Or pick whatever brings you freedom.

5. Go back and read the things you are grateful for. Can you add more? If so, add more things or people you are grateful for. Convert anger or unforgiveness you've had to gratitude and write those down.

**TURNING UP THE FIRE HERE!**

Take some time out to talk to your partner about these things, but first start with what you're grateful for and what you appreciate in your spouse. Then ask them if you can share what has hurt you and let your spouse know you forgive them. You also need to ask your partner to share how you've hurt them and ask them to forgive you.

<u>4 Key Points to this Discussion to **LOVE**</u>

1. Let the conversation be non-defensive and open-minded, this is not a finger pointing or yelling moment. This is a time to share how you each feel without any retaliation. "We all have the right to feel what we feel, it doesn't make our feelings right." So keep in mind that our feelings can be deceiving and when you are open to listen, you may learn that you had every right to feel the way you did, but your feeling may have been based on a falsehood.

2. **O**perate with compassion and empathy. Make sure it's a good time to talk. If you think it'll never a good time because you're in such a bad place with your partner, when it's quiet, just let them know, "I've been working on me, I realize that I needed to forgive you for anything you've ever done that made me feel hurt and I hope you can forgive me for anything I've done to hurt you, because I'm sorry."

    If you find a good time, let them know you have some things on your mind and heart that you'd like to discuss. **ASK** them if it's a good time to talk and be specific about how much time you need. **WHY** ask and give a specific time, because you want to go into a sensitive topic with guards down and you want to show respect from the beginning of this conversation. Your relationship may be very guarded now due to all the pain, so until there is an understanding and change, you should go into difficult conversations with permission and respect for how they may feel. **WAIT** for your partner to say yes to having the conversation. Forcing someone to talk about any topic will not have positive results. Be mindful of the time you decided to have conversation. It can be easy to go down a rabbit hole and stir ill feelings, causing the conversation to go bad. Stick to the list and let go, forgive. Having empathy helps you to try to understand why they felt the way the felt, whether right or wrong.

If your partner says no to having the conversation, then this is where you go back to letting them know "I've been working on me, I realize that I needed to forgive you for anything you've ever done that made me feel hurt and I hope you can forgive me for anything I've done to hurt you, because I'm sorry."

3. **Vulnerability** will take you further than you ever thought. Tear down the walls, free yourself from your prison, and talk openly. This will begin to build a strong foundation that's clear for your journey forward.

4. Every day, practice forgiveness with yourself and your partner, have the conversations, operate with compassion and empathy, and be vulnerable.

*Love Tip!*

*Men do better when they are not caught off guard with a hard conversation. They also do better when they know they are not going to be caught in an hour-long conversation or argument. They just want to get to the point and be done with it…work with him.*

### MEET SOMEWHERE IN THE MIDDLE

*Women want to have long conversations and explain every detail to what happened and why. This makes them feel connected and understood better when they are listened to…work with her.*

## **Check-In**

**How do you feel right now?**

_____

_____

_____

_____


**Is there anything you feel you haven't let go of?**

_____

_____

_____

_____

*Be sure to take more time if needed to process anything you may still be holding on to & practice forgiveness!*

*Time Out!*
*Breathe and Be Still.*

> *"Be still and know that I am God,"*
> *Psalm 46:10*
>
> *(New International Version(NIV))*

## *Forgive Others!*

Sometimes we don't realize how our childhood or other people affect our marriage. Parents, friends, co-workers, our children, in-laws, past relationships...they have all affected us. When you harbor unforgiveness toward anyone, it breaks you down and hurts your relationships. Some of these people you will be able to actively meet with and have the same conversation you had with your spouse, some you may never speak to again. Either way, you want to go through the same process you went through for yourself and your spouse. If it's possible, you want to let them know you forgive them, ask them to forgive you, and move forward!

First things first, gratitude! Think about what you are grateful for in the people in your life. This could be anyone but focus on those who have hurt you and you have not forgiven. It may be for the way they served you at some point, how they helped you grow through the pain, or for simply for teaching you how not to be. Write your list here.

***I am grateful for*** _____ ***because:*** (Write their name and what you're grateful for):

_____

_____

_____

_____

_____

_____

_____

_____

_____

_____

_____

_____

_____

_____

_____

*Yes, I know this is some hard stuff! If this is not hard for you...DIG DEEPER! True lasting change happens when you can be real, raw, and vulnerable. This is necessary for your breakthrough and transformation.* On the next page, write out anything/everything you need to forgive them for.

## "Forgive It" or "F It" List

I Have Not Forgiven You,_____, for…
(write their name and what hurt you)

_____

_____

_____

_____

_____

_____

_____

_____

_____

**BUT TODAY, RIGHT NOW, I FORGIVE YOU FOR IT ALL!**
Do this even if they have not asked for your forgiveness!

## *Forgive Others!*

Now that you have written out your list of things you have not forgiven others for, read it to yourself and forgive them.

1. Tell yourself, "I forgive (their name or Them All) for it all!"
2. Take responsibility for hurts you may have caused, change that behavior in you, and forgive them for their part. If you need to, read each item and tell yourself, "I forgive them!" Use names if you need to have full release.
3. Identify things that are lies, bring them into the light, and speak truth into your heart, mind, body, and soul. Forgive Them!
4. Now cut or rip out the "Forgive It or F It List" page. Put this page aside for now. This step of ripping this page out or cutting it out symbolizes you removing unforgiveness from your life. As you rip it out, say, "F It!" Or pick whatever brings you freedom.
5. Go back and read the things you were grateful for. Can you add more? If so, add more things or people you are grateful for. Convert anger or unforgiveness you've had to gratitude and write those down.

Forgiving yourself and others, following the steps, is so important. If you don't forgive, if you don't move past the hurt, if you don't move forward...you will be stuck forever. You will repeat the same cycle and patterns your entire life. Dear Friend, it's not worth it. My life used to feel like a hamster wheel, but I wanted to be free. So I had to forgive myself, I had to forgive my ex-husband, I had to forgive my husband, my parents, my children, and others around me. I wanted freedom and want that for you too! Honestly, forgiveness is the only way to be free. So much of what we hold on to really isn't even worth the fight.

# Check-In

**How do you feel right now?**

_____

_____

_____

_____

_____

**Is there anything you feel you haven't let go of?**

_____

_____

_____

_____

_____

Is there anything you feel you cannot forgive? If so, what can you put in place to help you go through the process to forgive? (for example: seek counseling or connect with others who have experienced the same thing and have forgiven)

_____

_____

_____

_____

_____

_____

_____

_____

*Time Out!*

*Breathe and Be Still.*

*Bear with each other and forgive one another if any of you has a grievance against someone. Forgive as the Lord forgave you.*

*Colossians 3:13*

*(New International Version(NIV))*

*If we confess our sins, he is faithful and just and will forgive us our sins and purify us from all unrighteousness.*

**1 John 1:9**

*(New International Version (NIV)*

*Lovework: Thoughts and goals on forgiveness.*

## DESTROY THE "F IT LIST!"

Now you get to pick a method to destroy your "F It List." My personal favorite method of destroying the "F It List" is burning it. Other methods include shredding it, ripping it and then burning the pieces, running over it with a car… you can be creative! Pick a method that will bring total satisfaction and is safe. Whatever you do, BE SAFE in your destruction method! Celebrate! Throw your hands up in the air, dance, do whatever gives you a sense of empowerment and freedom, do it as that list burns or shreds or as you rip it to pieces. This will be your anchor for each time you want to hold on to something. This anchor will keep you in a place of practicing forgiveness.

An anchor is used to keep a vessel from drifting. Watching your "F It List" be destroyed can serve as an anchor. When you feel yourself drifting into the ocean of unforgiveness, go back to that moment, go back to throwing your hands up in the air, that dance, or whatever you did to empower you to freedom and release. Do whatever it takes to remind yourself to never go back to holding onto hurt and pain. When you destroy the list, you anchor your heart in truth and the practice of forgiveness. Letting go of the past and moving forward in love, you will break free from the bad habits of the past. Be Free, Dear Friend!

**How do you feel right now?**

_____

_____

_____

_____

_____

***I am so grateful for…***

_____

_____

_____

_____

_____

*Be self-aware of your conditions and expectations, when you Love.*

# 2

## Unconditional Love

*Become aware of your expectations.*

Love without conditions, without expectations, and without rules is the purest form of love. Conditional love is not real love; conditional love is about trying to control your environment and people in your life. This is usually an attempt to protect yourself. Love is about an understanding and respect for what each person wants and desires in their life. Do not confuse conditional love with setting healthy boundaries in your love life. Setting healthy boundaries is about understanding who you are, what you love, who/what you believe in, what you desire, who you want to be in life, and why. When you know who you are, then you can share this with those you love, and have an understanding with healthy boundaries.

Let's break this down. Years ago it bothered me that my husband would not fix things or do house projects in a timely manner. My dad was good at starting and finishing projects and he would not stop until it was done. I remember when I was 12 years old and my dad was replacing the shingles on our roof, and I was up on the roof helping him until the late hours in the night holding the light for him and handing him tools. My husband on the other hand would rip out the ceiling in our kitchen after a leak and we would go years with exposed beams in our kitchen. This drove me crazy. So I started calling my dad to come over and fix things around the house. That in turn drove my husband crazy. I had an expectation of my husband to get projects done no matter what it took, even if it meant late nights on a rooftop. My husband expected me to let him handle it in his time. These expectation caused many days of anger, arguments, and frustrations.

To simplify things, don't have expectations in your relationships. Understanding the person you love will lead to you giving each other what you each desire and want in your relationship. You may struggle with the thought of not having expectations and some say that "realistic expectations" are acceptable. But who determines what is realistic? I used to believe that "common sense" was something everyone acquired. I have come to learn that this is based on what each individual views as "common." Therefore, what is "common" to me, may not be "common" for you. In the same way, what's "realistic" to you may not be "realistic" for me. When we eliminate the expectation altogether, then we can replace it with an understanding of who we are and agree to honor and respect that.

Years later, my husband and I now have an understanding of the things we desire. We have taken the time to get to know each other better. We have asked questions and listened to the answers. My husband shared with me how he felt disrespected when I brought my father in to fix things around the house. He simply wanted me to ask him if he needed help and allow him the opportunity to ask my father himself. He also wanted me to be clear on a realistic timeline for him to complete projects around the house. His desire was to please me and do the things that needed to get done and the things I wanted. I shared with him how I desired to have a home that felt like a safe haven, a calm space that I felt comfortable in. Therefore, when things looked ugly or undone, I felt uneasy. When we were clear on our desires and things we loved and who we were and wanted to be for ourselves and each other, this created healthy boundaries.

The problem starts when you aren't clear on who you are and what you desire. If you don't know who you are and what you desire, you can't know the person who you are with and what they desire on the deepest level. You get in a relationship and settle for what you get. I'm not talking about having a condition or expectation, but when you enter a relationship and both understand each other; then you will desire to give unconditional love, regardless of what you get because you fully understand what you came in to. Develop that healthy understanding of who you are, what you stand for, and from there you can develop relationships with people that understand, honor, and respect you with healthy boundaries.

*₄ Love is patient, love is kind. It does not envy, it does not boast, it is not proud. ₅ It does not dishonor others, it is not self-seeking, it is not easily angered, it keeps no record of wrongs. ₆ Love does not delight in evil but rejoices with the truth. ₇ It always protects, always trusts, always hopes, always perseveres. ₈ Love never fails.*

*1 Corinthians 13: 4-8*
*(New International Version (NIV)*

# Lovework
# Foundation to Self-Love & Self- Awareness

Who are you and do you love yourself?

_____

_____

_____

_____

_____


Who are you spiritually, who do you feel God has called you to be: are you a prayer warrior, a messenger?

_____

_____

_____

_____

_____

_____

Are you becoming all you desire? If yes, how? If not, who do you want to become? (Family, Health, Career, Success)

_____

_____

_____

_____

_____

_____

Where do you want to be? (Live, work, travel, etc.)

_____

_____

_____

_____

_____

_____

Who do you want to be with or do life with?

_____

_____

_____

_____

_____

Why do you desire all the above?

_____

_____

_____

_____

_____

Is there anything or anyone that your feel blocks you from Self-Love?

_____

_____

_____

_____

_____

What changes do you need to make to unblock self-love?

_____

_____

_____

_____

_____

## **Lovework**

**What do you desire from your spouse and Why?**

# How will you share your desires with your spouse?

**What do you desire from the other relationships in your life? (family, friends, co-workers, boss, business partner)**

How will you share your desires with the other relationships in your life? (family, friends, co-workers, boss, business partner)

**Identify healthy boundaries you need to set in your relationships and share them with your spouse and others.**

## *Remove Negative Influence*

When I began learning more about women's empowerment, my relationship suffered. My pursuit to be a stronger woman affected how I loved my husband. I love having a masculine powerful man, but I allowed the outside influence of women empowerment to affect this desire I had in a negative way. I developed this unrealistic expectation of being a powerful woman to a powerful man and couldn't understand why there was conflict. The two can exist together but not at the same time.

When my husband took on the role of Father or Protector of our home, this was not the time for me to step in and interrupt his power because I was powerful too. We could never have 2 Presidents of the United States, but we think we can have 2 Alpha leaders in our home. We each have a role in life and sometimes our roles change or switch. We need to master the role we are in each moment. At times, my husband is the powerful masculine man and the leader. At other times, however, I can assert my power, and my husband adjusts to follow me. This is something we do naturally; I don't think about switching roles, I just do.

## *Pursue Unconditional Love*

However, when there is conflict, we need to be self-aware of our role.

I always had something to say or input on everything, I was breaking my husband down and belittling him as a man. I also talked to people who encouraged me not to "put up with stuff." So I'd find myself having an attitude the moment I felt challenged by anyone. Take the guard down, put the guns down, tear down the walls. When you're always waiting to go in and fight/go to war or have resistance, that is exactly what you will get. Then we may wonder why you're always arguing. We may do this because we've been hurt and want to protect ourselves, when we're really only hurting ourselves and those around us. In the same way, there were things my husband did that were hurtful to me. In his role as "the man of the house," at times he was harsh, it was his way or no way. Culturally, being a Puerto Rican male, some may say, "this is how they roll." This was "common sense" to him. Then you add fifteen plus years in the military and orders were being made on a constant basis. But I wasn't having it, that was not realistic to me. Now being a Puerto Rican female, raised by a strong, vocal Puerto Rican mother who took on more of the Alpha role in our home…we had conflict! Our resistance against each other only caused us to build walls up as a form of protection and resistance to surrender. This caused us both to begin to shut down in our relationship. We began to lose love, honor, and respect for each other.

Addiction can be another negative influence. You can be addicted to a TV show that takes you away from people you love, a substance you abuse, pornography that creates unrealistic expectations, another person you're attracted to, or games you love playing. Do not confuse this with the importance of having time for yourself and doing things you enjoy in a controlled manner. You may love a show that you watch weekly and have that time for yourself, however, when that begins to interrupt or cause conflict because now you binge watch the show daily, ask yourself, "Do I have balance in my life with my time?"

## *Be Aware of Negative Influences!*

Look at your love life, (not the one in bed, although you could consider that one too) and the way in which you love. Has it been conditional or unconditional? Once you've gone through each step of knowing who you are, becoming self-aware, and removing negative influences, now it's time to remove the conditions of your love. Start to recreate your love and your understanding with your loved ones, your spouse, children, and others in your life. Be determined to tear down the walls of conditions and expectations and live a life of freedom!

## *With forgiveness and unconditional love, your life will begin to transform!*

Forgiveness and unconditional love are the foundation of your love for yourself, then in turn for others. You can love yourself unconditionally, when you have gone through the process of understanding you, and then love others unconditionally.

# Reality Check!

## *Unconditionally love yourself, your spouse, and others.*

Become self-aware of what you do (your actions) that tell you or others the conditions of your love for them, meaning, you love IF_____. (Fill in the blank). Some of my conditions were, I love you IF I get my way, I love you IF I'm happy, I love you IF you say what I want to hear. When you realize that many times conditions on our love is our way of controlling someone and that is not love, we can begin to transform our mindset toward love.

What conditions have you placed on your love, for yourself? Have there been times that you flipped out on yourself for not doing something you wanted to do, maybe you talked yourself out of it because of fear. Do you judge yourself harshly? (For example: When I lose 10lbs then I'll feel better about how I look. When I get the promotion or higher paying job, then I'll feel better about my life.)

_____

_____

_____

_____

_____

Why did you create these conditions for yourself? Consider did someone hurt you, by making a statement that caused you to believe these things about you? Have you forgiven them?

___

What conditions have you placed on your love for your spouse? Ask your spouse if they feel you have placed conditions on your love for them.

___

Think of times that you've overreacted, flipped out, or judged your spouse for one reason or another; write them down. This may help uncover some hidden conditions of your love. Ask your spouse to share times that they have felt you were hard on them or that they felt unloved. Conditions on love make people feel unloved or they may feel used. Write down what your spouse shares.

_____

_____

_____

_____


What conditions have you placed on your love for others? Ask your children or those close to you if they feel you have placed conditions on your love for them.

_____

_____

_____

_____

Think of times that you've overreacted, flipped out, or judged the people in your life for one reason or another; write them down. This may help uncover some hidden conditions of your love for them. Ask them to share with you times that they have felt you were hard on them or that they felt unloved. Write down what they share.

_____

_____

_____

_____

There are people or things around you that influence your love for yourself, your spouse, or others. (Examples: someone you're attracted to, music, people who don't support your love life/who you love, anything you're addicted to: games, porn, shows, etc.) What are these things for you?

_____

_____

_____

_____

_____

How will you put distance or completely stop associating or participating with those people or things that are a negative influence on you? Remember, you have the power and will to make this decision. The more you continue to decide to do what is best, the easier it gets.

_____

_____

_____

_____

_____

_____

_____

_____

_____

_____

_____

_____

*₁₈ There is no fear in love. But perfect love drives out fear, because fear has to do with punishment. The one who fears is not made perfect in love.*

*1 John 4:18*
*New International Version (NIV)*

Now that you have a list of how you love, a list of conditions you've had, a list from your spouse's/partner's point of view (if available), others' viewpoint, and a list of things or people that negatively influence your love, it's time to decide *what you need to keep doing, not do, do less or more of* when it comes to loving yourself/spouse/others.

One of my examples is realizing how music was influencing my marriage and my love for my husband. I needed to stop listening to certain kinds of music. I would listen to soul music that expressed lots of sadness and women empowerment. Which isn't necessarily a bad thing except when you're already in a bad place and easily influenced. Many of the songs were strong women who did life alone or found the strength to do things themselves. As I mentioned, this music can be wonderful depending on where you are in your life. In my case, as I struggled in my marriage, I felt empowered to leave my husband because I was unhappy rather than work on it. I struggled with depression, I was angry and bitter, therefore this music only exacerbated my already difficult situation. There were people I needed to limit my interactions with because they did not represent me or what I wanted my relationship to reflect. Being aware of the negative influences and things you need to stop doing are two crucial exercises. Being intentional about your influences and actions can save you and your relationships from much pain, divorce, or losing a job or a friend.

Identifying areas we need to change or things we need to stop doing can improve our relationships. Our loved ones see, know, and feel when we respond in love, in arrogance, in a sarcastic way, or anger. I realized I was demeaning my husband and then wondered why he was demeaning me. Remember, as the saying goes, "hurt people, hurt people." I was demeaning my husband by calling my dad to help me with work that needed to be done in the house, I would talk about him to my sisters, negatively sharing my frustrations about him. These were things that minimized him as my husband, as a man who tried, and while he had things to work on, my choosing to respond in this way did not help.

Temptation could come in, to go outside of your marriage to seek love or attention elsewhere. During moments of weakness, someone will come into your life and give you attention, speak to you in a way that makes you feel amazing, respected, loved, or makes you feel safe...now the door is open for infidelity. When you are not meeting a need for love, connection, significance, or certainty, there will be an attraction to people or things that do fulfill those needs. For men it may be their need for love or significance, and they want it through respect, sex, or affection...they may become attracted to a woman who has these qualities. Women may be drawn to a man that takes the lead (if your husband does not), or a man who makes us feel safe or loved, to fulfill a need for certainty and connection. I was unfaithful because I needed to feel loved. I allowed myself to find comfort in someone else in my weakest moment.

Because of my expectations, negative influences, resentment, and the walls I built, I cheated on my first and current husband. I justified my actions in my first marriage by saying it happened once after ten years of pain, lies, and many other things. In my marriage now, I justified my infidelity at the time by thinking this man never protected me, wanted to control me, never listened to me, and I felt alone. Both times I let my guard down and *I allowed the appearance that someone else cared get the best of me…or really the worst of me!*

The choices we make that negatively impact our marriage and relationships bring shame, they silence us, and we basically crawl back into a box and cannot live to our fullest potential. I wasted too much time, even after I had confessed what I had done to my husband, living in fear and shame. I was afraid people would not like me or accept me if they knew what I had done. Here was a well-established man that people would say was crazy for marrying a woman with four children from a previous marriage. I then felt that they were right because I hurt him in the worst way. I wanted to live under a rock and not live out my calling to help restore marriages. But the lies and the stories we tell ourselves keep us living in pain and repeating the same cycles that destroy us.

As I began to speak my truth, regardless of how ugly and shameful it was, I began to realize that it no longer mattered who liked me, who hated me, who criticized me, because I knew who I was, who I was called to be, what I needed to do, and that I would be able to help many. When you free yourself from unforgiveness, learn to love unconditionally, remove the false expectations, and ignore what others say or what we think others will say, life gets so much easier.

When you can love unconditionally, it means you love even when you don't like what is done or said...you can still love and respond in love. (Don't confuse this with an abusive relationship, which is always unacceptable.) In spite of what I had done, my husband chose to love me unconditionally! This did not mean he was not hurt, it did not mean I was not hurt, we needed time to heal ourselves and our relationship. However, when we both took responsibility for what we did wrong in our relationship and we stopped pointing the finger at each other...we fell in complete and total love, like never before! I went from not being able to stand being around this man, to hating being without him.

# Lovework

## *What Love Feels Like To You...*

What makes you feel loved? Think of words you love to hear, things you love to do, to receive, to physically feel, and write them all down.

_____

_____

_____

_____

What does your spouse do to make you feel loved and does it match what you said?

_____

_____

_____

_____

How often does your spouse do things that make you feel loved? Would you love it if they did it more, if yes, how often?

_____

_____

_____

_____

_____

Ask your spouse what makes them feel loved, what they love to hear, things they love to do, to receive, physically feel, and write them all down.

_____

_____

_____

_____

_____

What do you do to make your spouse feel loved? Does it match what they said?

How often do you do the things that make them feel loved? Would they love it if you did it more, if so, how often?

Is there another important relationship that needs to feel your love, if so, who?

Ask them what would make them feel loved by you, what you can do, say, physically do, or give to them to show your love for them. How often do you need to do this?

# *Check-In*

**How do you feel right now?**

 

**Are there conditions or expectations you are struggling to let go of?**

Are there conditions or expectations you feel you cannot let go of? If so, how can you change those expectations to healthy boundaries or desires?

_____

_____

_____

_____

_____

_____

_____

_____

_____

*Time Out!*

*Breathe and Be Still.*

*P.S. Like most things, unconditional love is something you practice daily. It's also a choice. Decide today, right now, to love people where they are, to love them despite their flaws and imperfections, and most importantly believe the best in them. You have them in your life for a reason, you must believe they love you or are good for you; otherwise why are we even talking about them? You have chosen to have them in your life, now choose to love them without condition.*

# *I am grateful for...*

# 3
# Communication

*Listen & Speak in a way they feel loved.*

I remember when my communication started to break down in my marriage. It seemed like one day everything I said bothered him and everything he said bothered me. However, someone else could come along and say the exact same thing and it was GOLD. The first time I remember this happening was when our daughter was born at 25 weeks. She spent 3 months in the Newborn Intensive Care Unit (NICU). I would go see her every day. She was my 5th child and Carlos' 1st. Her first two months of life were touch and go. He would come see her a few times per week and if I tried to help him care for her, he didn't want to hear it. While I just wanted to protect our baby, he just wanted to figure it out on his own. He would change her diaper and since she had a breathing tube we couldn't lift her too high or it would cut the oxygen to her lungs, so I would remind him to lower her legs. This was the beginning of many communication breakdowns. He would get upset with me and tell me to let him figure it out. But the nurse would see him and let him know he needed to lower her legs and he would thank her.

So I slowly said less and less, and I didn't want to listen to him either. I believed my delivery was kind in the way I communicated, so I couldn't understand why his response to me was so negative. Remember that dig deep Lovework of forgiveness and unconditional love? Years later, after going through this process, I realized that his negative responses to me were reinforcing my feelings of not being good enough. He didn't know this, neither did I. But I felt like I wasn't good enough unless I did something to make him happy (conditional love). He didn't realize that he was reinforcing the negative feelings I already had.

The most important part of communication is how you listen, because when you listen first, your response can be more understanding and grace-filled. When we don't listen and have a response for someone before they're even done speaking, our response is usually selfish and self-centered. Keep in mind that at times, we have established our way of communication with our loved ones and it may be a defensive or confrontational type of communication. People may respond to us based on the form of communication we've established. If you're always defensive or argumentative, then you may find people in your life are always ready for confrontation with you or avoid you altogether. If you have established communication that has no emotion, you may find people's conversations with you are very shallow.

Take some time to identify how you communicate and what form of communication you have established in your relationships.

**₁₉ Understand this, my dear brothers and sisters! Let every person be quick to listen, slow to speak, slow to anger.**

*James 1:19*

*New English Translation (NET Bible)*

# **Foundation to Communication**

When was your communication at its best?

_____
_____
_____
_____

When did your communication start to break down? What was happening? If you've had great communication, what has made it great?

_____
_____
_____
_____

Ask your spouse/partner where they feel your communication is weak or could use work or has totally broken down. Or you can identify when your communication was poor and what caused it.

_____

_____

_____

_____

Now that you've identified areas where your communication is poor or broken, take each area and think of how you can change the communication in a positive way. Write down new loving responses to the negative ways you've communicated in the past to begin to change how you'll communicate moving forward.

_____

_____

_____

_____

# **Couple's Lovework**

*Go through this section individually and then with love and guards down, discuss together.*

What are things you know and practice that are wonderful about your love and communication?

_____
_____
_____
_____
_____

What are things you know are not great about the way you love and communicate, that you will no longer do? _____

_____
_____
_____
_____
_____

What do you believe caused your communication to break down? _____

_____

_____

_____

_____

_____

_____


How will you begin to rebuild and recreate the broken areas of your communication?

_____

_____

_____

_____

_____

_____

*Listen, don't just hear what is being said.*

To actively listen to someone is the most important part of communication, along with listening without judgment. I have struggled with this. As I have worked through this, I have come to realize how judgmental I can be. I've also learned that when I do listen without judgement, I hear things differently. What does all this mean?

My definition of hearing is sound that enters the ears, produces noise and is heard.

vs.

My definition of listening is to hear the sound or words and understand what is being said.

**My definition of communicating with love is to listen and respond in a non-judgmental and non-defensive way.**

Here is an example of a situation where I could have heard what was said vs. listened and then what my response would have been to each one.

When I have had disagreements with my husband, here are ways I could have heard him or listened to him with my example responses for each:

| Spouse Statement | My thoughts based on what I heard... | What I communicate after hearing | My thoughts based on when I listen... | What I communicate after listening |
|---|---|---|---|---|
| "I need you to stop spending money. The budget is tight and we don't have extra money to spend, you have to stick to the budget." | I'll stop "wasting" money on buying enough food for the house, paying for kids' school expenses, and my occasional trip to nail salon that you obviously don't think I deserve. | So what you spend money on is more important than me and the kids... Got It! | Finances are tight and he wants to care for our family and provide. He's concerned bills won't get paid and we need to talk about expenses more clearly so he understands when and why I spent additional money. | Thank you for caring for our family and providing. I agree I need to be mindful of expenses. Can we review what I have spent money on to determine what I can eliminate? |

How many times do you get defensive when your spouse points something out? Do you believe your spouse sees the worst in you and is not looking out for you? If you believe they do not have your best interest at heart, either you're believing a lie or have a lot of work to do. As you listen, remind yourself that they want the best for me, I want the best for them, they love me, I love them, they're helping me grow, and I want to help them. Then you have practiced communicating in love and the interaction has begun in a positive way. If they do not have your best interest at heart, then the bigger question is why and why are they in your life?

## *Communicate, don't leave them guessing.*

What do you want? Tell them. You then need to be clear and let your thoughts be known. Letting your thoughts, feelings, and desires known in a loving way; not in a defensive, interrogating, or harsh way, is important. This goes back to having an understanding. And even if you have established an understanding in your relationship of what you desire, sometimes our feelings and desires change. Okay, so you may be thinking this is too much to process or think about. You may even think it's just easier to left things unsaid. And there *are* things that are better left unsaid. Let's break that down. There are times that our children will misbehave and my husband may correct them differently than I would, or as I would think, more harshly. Sometimes I've believed that my children are acting or reacting the way my husband would and I used to say, "Look at the pot calling the kettle black!" Of course, this would only get a reaction out of my husband and it was really unnecessary. It was unnecessary because my husband loves our children and he wants the best for them. Therefore, this was a time I needed to support him in his correction for their good, not put his correction down by criticizing him. However, for those things that need to be said, do so and do it with love. In this case with the misbehaving children, I could have spoken to him at a later time and asked him if I could give him feedback on the children's behavior. I also believe there are some responsibilities that are shared and I always believe we should take personal responsibility first. Therefore, I needed to first start with identifying ways I could be a better example to the children and identify a specific incident where they may have been responsible for an unwanted behavior also. Offer to hold each other accountable to being better examples and having more grace when correcting behaviors. Don't assume your loved ones know or should know by now.

Remember, even if you think something is common sense or they should just know…don't assume they remember or know. Be willing to repeat yourself with grace. There are times we hear what is being said but we don't listen. Even if you think he should know, tell him again. Changing the way you communicate will feel so awkward at first. It will almost feel fake but if you truly want to change things in your relationship for the better, you will need to do things that are different or even uncomfortable. You may have been raised in a home where yelling or harsh communication was the norm. How did that work in your home then? This is a whole other relationship, your spouse is not your dad, your mom, or your brother. It comes down to having faith that the more you do the right thing and respond in the right way, your relationship will begin to get stronger, you will repair the brokenness, and begin to find a deep love you've never had before. *First step to change anything, is to realize change needs to happen.*

## *Faith It Til You Make It!*

I have always been a big believer in "putting your big girl/boy pants on" and "suck it up" and just deal with whatever comes at us. I have had to understand that while we should not live in a victim mentality and wallow in self-pity, we need to have grace. Grace means having balance in the way we communicate and in what we communicate. We need to be aware of what form of communication works best for those we love. I grew up in a great, imperfect home where yelling was normal, but my husband did not have the same level of loudness I had. What may be normal communication for me feels like yelling for him. Be aware of your partner's form of communication that serves them best and be willing to practice it daily with them.

Let's face it, we are not always on our A-Game. We all have bad days and days that we don't want to be bothered with worrying about anyone but ourselves. And that is okay, as long as every day is not all about us. Just the same way you don't want to deal with someone else having a constant pity party, be self-aware if you're always the one with the pity party. When you work through recreating your love, it starts with taking responsibility for ourselves, our actions, and then moves into serving others on a high level through forgiveness, unconditional love, healthy communication, and the other areas you will work on in this book. If your heart is willing, I commend you Dear Friend. If your heart is resistant, I encourage you to take a leap of faith and give this a chance.

## *Check-In*

How do you feel right now?

Are there areas that you are doing more hearing vs. listening? If so, how will you change that and begin to respond with love?

**Is there anything you still feel you will struggle with in your communication? If so, what will you put in place to help you communicate better?**

_____

_____

_____

_____

_____

_____

_____

_____

_____

*Time Out!*

*Breathe and Be Still.*

> "You are the average of the five people you spend the most time with."
>
> — Jim Rohn

# *I am so grateful for...*

# 4

## Self-Control

### *The Power of the Mind!*

I love to watch movies that portray a wonderful love story, two of my favorites are Dirty Dancing and Brown Sugar. Dirty Dancing was the first movie Carlos and I watched together back in 1993, our first date. This young privileged girl falls in love with an older hotel worker, with the leather jacket, who's somewhat perceived as a "bad guy," but he really has a good heart and who can forget the dance talent. Brown Sugar is all about childhood friends who love music and each other, but go their separate ways, then find their way back to each other. Both movies end with them openly expressing their love for each other and seem to live happily ever after. And yes, I love the ones that are so predictable: they fall in love, go through some hardship, and find their way back to each other (it reminds me of my story). If we think about it, it's just the average love story on some level or another. Most of us fall in love, go through challenges, and either break up or work it out. But we can get so caught up in a good love story and forget about reality. If we're not careful, this is where we can develop those conditions on our love life and then lack control on our image of love. When you begin to compare yourself or your relationship to the ones you see on TV or on Social Media; you slowly kill off parts of your own relationship; if not all of it. In practicing self-control of your mind, remember that no one else's story or love life is perfect, and yours doesn't have to be perfect either.

## *The Joneses Don't Always Stay Together!*

Sadly, divorce rates in the U.S. have been as high as 50%! When we are surrounded by divorced family and friends, divorce may seem like a more comfortable answer to our problems. You need to take an inventory of your thoughts and actions when it comes to love and your relationships. Having control over our choices and decisions, despite what those around us are doing, is something we must be intentional about. At times, things are happening subconsciously and subtly. Be aware of your surroundings so you can set healthy boundaries, which lead to self-control when those negative conversations creep up. We need self-control in our communication, what we allow ourselves to see or believe, the negative influences or choices that could affect our relationships, and how we spend our time. These are a few, think of areas you can identify as areas you need to maintain self-control. Just a reminder, self-control does not mean passively accepting abuse; abuse is never part of a healthy relationship. When you or your partner makes a choice to not control any abusive action, in my opinion, separation needs to happen, and professional help sought out.

## **Reality Check on Self-Control & Your Mindset!**

Are there people that you compare yourself and/or your relationship too? If so, why, what attracts you to them?

_____

_____

_____

_____

Are there people or things that tempt you to go into a fantasy world or desire a life that is not your own? If so, who and/or what? Describe your fantasy or dream.

_____

_____

_____

_____

Where do you lack self-control? (Example: TV, food, gossip, excessive exercise, in work/business)

What healthy boundaries can you put in place to eliminate your lack of control in these areas?

What lies are you believing about your relationship/love? How can you change these?

We need to develop mental toughness and drive to pursue our relationships the same way we did in the beginning throughout the years we're together. As we live in a generation of instant gratification, self-control seems to be limited. Self-control is much easier when you surrender to the fact that life is not perfect, the people we love are not perfect, and we're all on a journey to live the most perfect life possible. When you accept this, then you can extend grace when things don't go your way. When you have self-control, you take the time to stop, think, and process situations before responding or reacting. Get control of your mind or your mind will control you.

## *Get Your Mind Under Control!*

Before my separation, I remember living in my head. I imagined myself in this great relationship, with a great man (not my husband, we had too much pain), and I imagined my kids done with school and out of the house. I was FREE! Or so I thought. I would go to my thoughts of this perfect world, every time I felt hurt, angry, or frustrated, and that happened often. I would find myself getting to places and not remembering how I got there. I would drive in a daze and realize I forgot where I was going…the life in my head was taking over me. This may sound crazy and it was. I was allowing my thoughts and my mind to take over me. Eventually my thoughts got me to cheat and live out some form of what was in my head, except it was nowhere near as perfect as my thoughts. In fact, it became more of a nightmare. I was used for anything but love and quickly realized…the grass was not greener.

I'm so grateful I reached a point that I decided not to allow another one of those thoughts to consume me any longer. I realized that lacking self-control in my mind robbed me from being present in the life I had and the moments with my kids, and that was not worth it, regardless of any pain I felt.

How did I stop using the thoughts in my head or my "imaginary life" as a go-to? How did I stop cheating? How did I stop listening to music that influenced me negatively? I practiced self-control. I stopped. When you truly want change, you will be willing to do anything! If you feel like you can't stop doing something, check your heart, do you honestly want to stop? That answer is simple...No! You are reading this because you want to change or improve your love life. Change starts with you. If you truly cannot stop doing something that you know needs to stop, then seek help. While I have heard of people who stop things cold turkey, I also understand we are all created differently. Therefore, seek help whether from a friend, a therapist, or accountability partner. Understand the insanity or fix what is not working by changing it.

And for you, it may not be your thoughts, it may not be the music you listen to, it may be the people you let get in your head, it may be the other man you're talking to that listens and understands you, it may be a beautiful woman who worships the ground you walk on, it may the shows you're watching on TV, it may be your attitude...whatever it is, separate and divorce that...now! Sadly, we're much quicker to divorce our spouse but not the toxic things that are killing our marriage. We didn't have cable for years because we knew we did not want to waste time watching TV or money.

We made conscious decisions of what we would watch and listen to.

I used to think, "But how do I just stop?" In a weird way, I just wanted to reach my happy ending in my head. That never came, was never going to come, and I just had to stop. Self-control is as powerful as forgiveness. And when you feel like you are not strong enough, pray or meditate! I used to talk to a man that God relocated across the country to save my marriage!!! If you don't believe in God, you must believe in something. Tap into your core beliefs and live them out. As the quote says, "If you don't stand for something, you'll fall for anything." When you decide that you want to change and you put your thoughts on those changes, things begin to happen. Change will happen! You will manifest what you think about whether good or bad, you have the power. But one thing is for sure, if you are doing things in a bad way, no matter how good your mind can imagine something, it will always end bad. You cannot manifest good where bad is involved. Clean up your act, better yet, clean up your mind and your actions. Practice self-control and watch your life transform, yet again.

## **Identify Problem(s) Areas or Where You Lack Self-Control**

Are you quick to quit when things get hard in your relationship, at work, in life in general? If so, why?

_____

_____

_____

_____

What are some of the areas you lack self-control/identify the problem areas?

_____

_____

_____

_____

**What** needs to change?

 

**Why** does this problem need to stop or change?

Identify the pain that it brings, if it continues.

What are the consequences of this problem/lack of control?

**Who** is affected if it continues? Is it worth it?

# *Check-In*

How do you feel right now?

_____

_____

_____

_____

Are there areas that you are lacking self-control? If so, how will you change that and begin to change that and gain control?

_____

_____

_____

_____

Is there anything you still feel you will struggle with in your self-control? If so, what help will you put in place to help you overcome this?

_____

_____

_____

_____

_____

_____

_____

_____

_____

_____

## *Time Out!*

## *Breathe and Be Still.*

## MAKE A DECISION

**How** will you stop or change your action or behavior that needs to stop or change?

_____

_____

_____

_____

_____


What specific steps will you take to stop the unwanted behavior or thoughts?

_____

_____

_____

_____

**When** will you stop/change? Give a specific date.

_____

_____

_____

_____

_____

**How** will your life look and feel when you change these things? Describe the joy, love, security, and growth you will feel and have.

_____

_____

_____

_____

_____

*Being specific about your goals and changes is important, right down to how it will make you feel. You want to connect with change on a deep level so that it sticks.*

[11] *"For **I** know the plans **I** have for you," declares the Lord, "plans to prosper you and not to harm you, plans to give you hope and a future."*

*Jeremiah 29:11*

*New International Version(NIV)*

# *I am so grateful for...*

# 5

## Reflect & Project

*Don't forget where you came from.*

Sometimes amid difficult times we forget why we fell in love or we don't see the many blessings we have in our lives. Reflecting on the past allows us to see how we have grown, where we can improve, or remember why we fell in love. Reflecting makes us unstoppable in our goal to love harder. The problems come when we get so focused on the negative thoughts, actions, or feelings that the negative mindset takes over. We start smiling and laughing less and less; we struggle with putting on that mask or fake smile when we're around other people. I knew it was bad when I made sure people saw I was not happy, however, no one ever asked me if I was. I remember going to church every Sunday and this was a place I would go in with a big smile on my face. While it was supposed to be a safe place where you connected with people, I learned it was where I was most fake. So I'd smile and act happy no matter what I was going through. Until my relationship was so broken down, that I was too tired to smile. I would walk in sad and leave sad and no one asked how I was doing. I would come home from work, my husband and kids were miserable or just worried about themselves, and no one asked how I was doing. People who were supposed to be closest to me no longer felt safe. That created more bitterness inside of me. This then caused me to detach from people around me. When we become disconnected, it becomes more dangerous.

This disconnection is the first sign that we are heading down the road to deep sadness or depression. If this is where you are today, not enjoying much, not smiling much, struggling to get out of bed, and questioning why living matters…talk to someone! Getting help is important to help you clear your head. There's nothing wrong with saying you need help. I was raised in a family that kept things private and we weren't supposed to talk about our personal problems to others. I was always the child that opened my big mouth and talked to people and I would get yelled at for doing so. But the reality is sometimes we struggle to remember why we fell in love, because we've stopped loving ourselves, we're depressed, and need help to get over those challenges.

Once you have some clarity and mental strength to reflect on all the good, the blessings, and the love you have, take some time to go through those happy memories and the reason you fell in love.

*Without reflection, we go blindly on our way, creating more unintended consequences, and failing to achieve anything useful.*

-Margaret J. Wheatley

## *Create a New Story.*

If there are bad memories that keep coming up, what lesson did you learn from that memory? How can you change the meaning of that memory and create a positive outcome to a negative situation?

> *Growing up, my birthday was never really celebrated because it was so close to Christmas. As an adult, I hated my birthdays because I connected my feeling loved and significant to my birthday celebration or the lack thereof. It felt like it was any other day. My sister had a birthday a month after me, she got a party and they would add me in when convenient. So again as an adult, when I felt like I was sharing my birthday with something or someone, it infuriated me. I had to disconnect my childhood from adulthood and my meaning I attached to a party or being celebrated. So now I know my parents did what they could and I honor them for that. I was always considered the tough one and didn't show much emotion, so they figured I could handle it and I could. They didn't love me any less. And as an adult, if I want a party, I will plan it for myself. However, letting go of that has allowed me to enjoy birthdays no matter what happens. I'm grateful each year for another year of life lived, I'm grateful for all my blessings, and if I want something special, I say it. I've changed the meaning.*

**Practice gratitude.** Reflecting on your blessings, big and small, will help strengthen your relationships. If you have dug a hole of despair and crawled into it, gratitude will help you climb out of this hole of hurt and sadness. While there are medical imbalances that may cause us to do things, we also have choices we can make, so take your power back wherever possible. Taking personal responsibility for the part we play, the decisions we make, and power we have is vital in developing healthy relationships with ourselves and others.

When you practice gratitude, you can't practice bitterness, anger, and hate at the same time. Take your mind off the negative and look at the things you have and are taking for granted. The fact that you can breathe and read this book right now is a blessing! You had a means of getting this book, even if it was free for you, you still had the ability to get access to it. There are so many people today that cannot get this book (or any book), they do not have the means, they may not be permitted to, or they may not even be able to read…BUT YOU DO! Stop and look around you, there is so much all around us that we can be grateful for. Take a deep breath in and out, close your eyes, feel the moment you are in right now and be grateful. Flooding your mind with good, thanksgiving, and positivity will allow you to feel full of life, regardless of what's going on around you.

## *Check-In*

What are the negative stories you're holding on to about yourself, that you need to change the meaning or the stories you've told yourself? (For example, "Growing up I was never loved in a positive way, bad things always happened, we were always broke, so that's not going to change now.")

_____

_____

_____

_____

_____

Is this an area you still struggle to have forgiveness and have not let go, if so, why?

_____

_____

_____

_____

_____

How will you move on and change this story? Plan it out with as many details as possible.

_____

_____

_____

_____

_____

What are the negative stories that you've told yourself about your spouse, that you need to change the meaning, or the stories you've told yourself about unhappy moments?

_____

_____

_____

_____

_____

Is this a story that you have struggled with letting go and forgiving? If so, why?

_____
_____
_____
_____
_____

How will you move on and change this story? Plan it out with as many details as possible.

_____
_____
_____
_____
_____

What are the negative stories that you've told yourself about other people in your life, that you need to change the meaning or the stories you've told yourself about them?

_____

_____

_____

_____

_____

Is this a story that you have struggled with letting go and forgiving? If so, why?

_____

_____

_____

_____

_____

How will you move on and change this story? Plan it out with as many details as possible. _____

_____

_____

_____

_____

_____

_____

_____

_____

_____

*Time Out!*

*Breathe and Be Still.*

## Lovework

### New Stories of Past Memories

**Reflections that have taught me, grown me, or pushed me to be who I want to be…**

**Reflection ~ I fell in love because…**

# Reflection ~ A special memory I have about my spouse…

## *Share your reflections with your partner.*

After your time of reflection, take time to reconnect with your partner and share things you've learn during this time. Share what you're grateful for in them.

## *Share your reflections with others.*

If there are people in your life that came up during your time of reflection, is there something you want to share with them? There could be someone who could really use your encouragement or connection with you.

## *Learn the Lesson.*

Reflection on your life may be very difficult for you, especially if you've experienced much pain, hardship, and failure. But I encourage you to reflect on the positive experiences more than the negative. Take the negative experiences and reflect on the lessons you learned from that time. If you feel like you did not learn anything from a difficult time, consider if that situation is a reoccurring situation. If it is, it's time to learn the lesson, unless you want to continue going through that same trial. Difficult times must teach us, or we find ourselves on that hamster wheel, going through the same thing over and over again. Remember the pain so you never go back there. But consider, if you have struggled to see the lesson in your pain or trials, have you taken personal responsibility? Maybe what happened to you was not your fault at all, but you can understand how other people's pain could cause them to hurt others. Learning the lesson doesn't excuse their action or how they hurt you, rather it gives you a greater understanding and teaches you an amazing level of forgiveness and grace. These are great reminders of the cross and how Christ died for our sins, forgiving us for all we've done, even if we didn't deserve it. Grace! Maybe this isn't you, you don't believe in God's grace through Christ Jesus. But have you ever done something and hurt someone in the process? Have you desired to be forgiven for something you did? Overall, remember forgiveness and learning this lesson, is for you!

## *I am so grateful for…*

# *Don't forget where you're going.*

**Project the life you want and set goals for your future.** Short-term and long-term goals are both important. Sometimes all we can plan for is today or this week and get through that, that's fine. But having goals will help us feel accomplished. Short-term goals are like fuel to help us keep going for our long-term goals. When we can look out into the future and envision the life we desire, we revive our mind, heart, body, and soul.

My husband gave me a prayer poem before our scheduled divorce date. It was titled, "Someone Better Than Me." He asked God in this prayer poem to bring me someone who was better than him, who would clean better, cook better, overall be better. This helped me to realize that he really did so much for me and he wanted to do much more for me. I was so busy focusing on what he wasn't doing. Deep down I knew he was the best for me and I was going to miss my best because I kept focusing on what I thought I was missing. This was not dismissing the areas that needed work, but simply peeling one layer at a time that helps us expose the good, giving us a chance to nurture and grow that positivity. Comparison has been a killer of many relationships, today more than ever with social media and people's lives being so visible. You have to guard your heart and your mind. Know who you are, what you want, and communicate that with your spouse.

Examine once again where you are now. Where do you want to be personally, spiritually, physically, and in your relationship? Rather than talking about what's not right, talk about what is and how you can make it better. I have learned over the years that when we can do more of the right thing and celebrate the good, the bad diminishes.

What personal short-term and long-term goals and dreams do you have for yourself?

_____

_____

_____

_____

_____

_____

_____

_____

_____

What goals and dreams have you both set together?

_____

_____

_____

_____

_____

What are your other goals? Think about your health, family, career, finances, hobbies, home, etc.

_____

_____

_____

_____

_____

## *Know where you're going.*

Take all the areas you have reflected on and consider where you want to be in 6 months, 1 year, 5 years, and 10 years. Having goals and reviewing them regularly helps us stay on track. When you have your target in front of you, it's much easier to hit the target. When you are not sure what your target is or you're shooting in the dark, chances are you're not going to get very far, if anywhere at all.

During our difficult times, my husband and I had very vague goals and most of them were so different. I felt like we weren't on different pages or even chapters, we were in totally different books. When we started setting new goals and tweaking old goals, we slowly started getting on the same book, then the same chapter, and many days we're even on the same page. The reality is, nothing is ever perfect. You are both two different people working on a common goal, to love each other the best way possible and do life together. It's okay to be in different places in life and that's where support comes in. Sometimes we just need to support our spouse in their goals and dreams, even if we don't align with them, which we'll explore in the next chapter. But before we go there, let's journal and set some L.O.V.E goals.

L - Legacy - How do you want to be remembered? What do you want to leave behind?

O - Owning - Own your life. Take control, make a commitment, and take responsibility! What will you change to pursue your goals more effectively?

V - Vision - Know your Vision, share it, pursue it, and make it happen.

E - Execute - Execute your plan to reach your goals and your vision. Own the life you want and are called to live, and build that legacy you want to leave.

*The plans of the diligent lead surely to abundance, but everyone who is hasty comes only to poverty.*

*Proverbs 21:5*
*New International Version(NIV)*

# L.O.V.E. Goals

## 6 Months

Goals I have for myself (dreams/health/purpose) are…

L_____

O_____

V_____

E_____

Goals I have for my marriage are…

L_____

O_____

V_____

E_____

Goals I have for my family/friends are…

L_____

O_____

V_____

E_____

Goals I have for my wealth (career/calling/success) are…

L_____

O_____

V_____

E_____


NOTES:

# If This...Then That!

If we don't accomplish these goals, I will feel...

I don't want to feel the pain of not accomplishing our goals so I will do these things to work toward our goals:

When we accomplish these goals, I will feel…

When we accomplish these goals, I will celebrate by…

# L.O.V.E. Goals

## 1 Year Goals

Goals I have for myself (dreams/health/purpose) are…

L_____

O_____

V_____

E_____

Goals I have for my marriage are…

L_____

O_____

V_____

E_____

Goals I have for my family/friends are…

L_____

O_____

V_____

E_____

Goals I have for my wealth (career/calling/success) are…

L_____

O_____

V_____

E_____

NOTES:

# If This...Then That!

If we don't accomplish these goals, I will <u>feel</u>…

_____

_____

_____

_____

_____


I don't want to feel the pain of not accomplishing our goals so I will <u>do</u> these things to work toward our goals:

_____

_____

_____

_____

_____

_____

When we accomplish these goals, I will <u>feel</u>...

When we accomplish these goals, I will <u>do</u> these things...

# L.O.V.E. Goals

## 5 Year Goals

Goals I have for myself (dreams/health/purpose) are…

L_____

O_____

V_____

E_____

Goals I have for my marriage are…

L_____

O_____

V_____

E_____

Goals I have for my family/friends are…

L_____

O_____

V_____

E_____

Goals I have for my wealth (career/calling/success) are…

L_____

O_____

V_____

E_____


NOTES:

# If This…Then That!

If we don't accomplish these goals, I will <u>feel</u>…

_____

_____

_____

_____

_____

I don't want to feel the pain of not accomplishing our goals so I will <u>do</u> these things to work toward our goals:

_____

_____

_____

_____

_____

When we accomplish these goals, I will _feel_...

_____

_____

_____

_____

_____

When we accomplish these goals, I will _do_ these things...

_____

_____

_____

_____

_____

_____

_____

# L.O.V.E. Goals

**10 Year Goals**

Goals I have for myself (dreams/health/purpose) are…

L_____

O_____

V_____

E_____

Goals I have for my marriage are…

L_____

O_____

V_____

E_____

Goals I have for my family/friends are…

L_____

O_____

V_____

E_____

Goals I have for my wealth (career/calling/success) are…

L _____

O _____

V _____

E _____


NOTES:

# If This...Then That!

If we don't accomplish these goals, I will <u>feel</u>...




I don't want to feel the pain of not accomplishing our goals so I will <u>do</u> these things to work toward our goals:

When we accomplish these goals, I will <u>feel</u>…

When we accomplish these goals, I will <u>do</u> these things…

Connecting your thoughts and feelings with your accomplishments, or even your thoughts of what failure would look like, can fuel you to reach the goals that you set out for yourself and your marriage. Review them at least twice a month (weekly is better). Adding this review to your weekly check in with your spouse will help you both stay on track to reach your goals.

If your spouse is not available, do it yourself. Always remember you can always work on you. The work you do on you will naturally flow into your relationship. If you find yourself not doing something, because your spouse "doesn't want to" or isn't putting any effort in, understand that you are pointing the finger and deferring. Even if there's truth in what you're saying or believing about your spouse, first thing is always taking personal responsibility and doing the work yourself with or without the support of others. You will project a much brighter future when you do the work yourself and point the finger at you first, see where you can change, grow, and set goals.

Understanding the definition of "Project" will bring some closure to this Chapter on reflection and projection. Looking up the formal definition to words is a great practice to have when trying to recreate or understand anything in life.

## Definition of Project

**project** <u>verb</u>
pro·ject | \ prə-'jekt
<u>How to pronounce project (audio)</u>
\
**projected; projecting; projects**
**Definition of** *project* **(Entry 2 of 2)**
*transitive verb*
1    a: to devise in the mind : DESIGN
       b: to plan, figure, or estimate for the future
2: to throw or cast forward : <u>THRUST</u>
3: to put or set forth: present for consideration
4: to cause to jut out
5: to cause (light or shadow) to fall into space or (an image) to fall on a surface
6: to reproduce (something, such as a point, line, or area) on a surface by motion in a prescribed direction
7: to display outwardly especially to an audience
8: to attribute (one's own ideas, feelings, or characteristics) to other people or to objects

https://www.merriam-webster.com/dictionary/project

*Consider the definition of "Project."*

*Take it in and understand what it means to project!*

# *I am so grateful for...*

# 6

## Believe

### *Believe in Yourself!*

I never realized how much I did not believe in myself until my late 30s. I had low self-esteem, although I thought my self-esteem was fine. I noticed that I was always worried about my weight, I worried about what other people thought about me, and I tried to put out a life of perfection. When I saw pictures of beautiful, skinny women, or saw a picture of myself, I'd feel fat. Some may call it body dysmorphia or perfectionism, but I began to see that I lacked a healthy view of myself. As I peeled back layers of my life, I was able to see how my relationship with my mother really set this "self-esteem" stage for me. I never felt like I was good enough, which caused me to always look to try and be good enough for anyone. So I was a yes girl, if anyone wanted anything, I'd say yes even if I wanted to say no. I started running away from home to please others, usually guys. As a teenager, I started having sex to feel accepted and because I didn't want to say no, or that would mean I'd make someone unhappy with me. I would self-harm to seek attention from others and forget the other parts of my life I felt pain. I was always looking for approval from others. Growing up, when I didn't get approval or a feeling of belonging, I rebelled. As an adult, guess what I did? When I didn't get approval from people, I rebelled: I quit jobs, I gave the silent treatment (which I mastered), I looked for new friends, and eventually I wanted a new husband.

I will never forget how my high school counselor told me I was not college material. My test scores in middle school were low, so she advised me to take business classes so I could just find a job out of high school. I told her I wanted to be a nurse. But she didn't listen, so I went on to take business high school classes. By my junior year I decided I didn't care what she said, I was going to college. I proceeded to double up on college prep classes my junior and senior year, setting me apart from my peers.

I went on to go to college and dropped out, got pregnant, and married (in that order). I eventually went back to college and received my bachelor's degree. Somewhere along the way, I started believing in myself. But after my first marriage failed, I felt myself on the hamster wheel of life again, running in this cycle of seeking to feel significant to people in my life. I didn't realize how selfish I was being as I was going through life always looking for what others could give to me. While I thought I was the most selfless person, I would do anything and everything for everyone and anyone…it was just my mask. The mask I wore was do, do, do in hopes that you get something in return, even though it was a desire to be appreciated and recognized, my approach was all wrong. I was so tired of feeling invisible to the world.

I wasn't connecting with others in a healthy way because I had lost my connection with myself. When I realized that this lack of connection was the root cause of my relationship problems, my life changed. When I began working through the steps of forgiveness, learning and having unconditional love, improving communication, having self-control over my thoughts and actions, and taking time to reflect and project, setting goals and taking action, my life began to be transformed! I finally began to BELIEVE in me. I redefined who I was and wanted to be.

What people thought of me no longer mattered. As I had clarity of who I was and what I wanted, I began believing in who I was becoming and who I had already been. I stopped allowing the person I was to be blinded by unforgiveness, guilt, and the lies I told myself and believed. I was buried under all the opinions and judgements of myself and the others. When I let go and moved forward, walking in my calling, my life changed. I was able to begin believing in my relationship and take my marriage to the next level. I was no longer in it for what I would get out of it, but I was in it because of what my calling and purpose was…to love hard regardless of what I got from it.

So let's do some deep diving in your belief system. What we believe drives so much of who we are, what we do, and why we do it. When you can understand what drives you, you will be able to understand others, and love on a deeper level. Understand that if you do not believe in yourself, it's almost impossible to truly believe in others. And if you do believe in yourself, go deeper. I have learned that my lack of commitment throughout my life, out of fear of rejection, affected my level of belief.

If you find yourself doing things for others that you aren't doing for yourself, then you are not fully committing to yourself. You may find that you avoid commitments because you're afraid you will not finish them or even worse, other people know you as the person who starts a billion things and never finishes anything. Being a person of your word to yourself and others is so important and determines your level of success in life and relationships.

***Believe in yourself and begin to feel what love really is.***

## *Check-In*

Do you believe in yourself? If yes, what does it look and feel like? If no, why?

_____

_____

_____

_____

Do you lack commitment to yourself? Do you say you'll do something and not do it for yourself?

_____

_____

_____

_____

How will you grow in this area?

Connect with your spouse or someone you trust. Discuss what you will do for yourself. How can your spouse help you?

## *Believe in Your Marriage!*

I will always remember when I told my husband I couldn't see our marriage working out and he said, "It's called faith." When we have faith, we believe in something we can't see, touch, smell, or hear. Faith is believing in something that you can't see, hear, or feel, but ***you are willing to believe without any true evidence of its existence***. Believing in your marriage will take your relationship to heights you've never been before. Not believing in your marriage will result in a miserable, unhappy life. Believing in your marriage goes hand in hand with believing in your husband. But they are different: when you believe in your marriage, you do not see it ending and when you believe in your spouse, you see them as the man or women who is already winning at life. Believe they are the man or woman for you, believe in who they are; whether they are the president of a big company, the trash collector of the dirtiest city, a security guard, or manager...BELIEVE THEY ARE YOUR KING OR QUEEN & TREAT THEM THAT WAY!

Looking back to my first marriage, my ex-husband and I did not believe in each other. I struggled to think that my ex-husband would change and maintain a consistent change. I believed he only believed in me when I made him happy. Our relationship was damaged and my heart was broken, and I never felt or heard him check in with me or try to pour love back into those broken areas. They remained broken. I had a miscarriage after my second child and while the pregnancy was unplanned, I was heartbroken. I remember sitting on the toilet the day after I had learned I was miscarrying and I talked to my dad and cried, as I passed my sweet baby. It wasn't until a few years ago, when I found myself thinking of my unborn baby around the time he or she would have been born, that I realized I had ignored how heartbroken I was over the loss. Men and women process things very differently and at the time my ex-husband processed that in a different way and that took away from my feelings of believing in him or our marriage.

I had a client who was constantly trying to make ends meet, working multiple jobs, and struggling for years. I remember asking how she and her spouse worked out their finances and she couldn't tell me. All she knew was that she had to give him a certain amount of money each paycheck, unsure what his income was, or how he contributed. For years she allowed resentment and disappointment to build in their marriage and she no longer believed in her husband or her marriage. Not every marriage can be saved, but the sooner you catch the lack of belief and the loss of faith in love for each other, the better chance you have to restore and rebuild a broken marriage.

When my husband and I decided to have faith and believe in our marriage, there was a shift and transformation began. About a year after we reunited, my husband told me he supported me in leaving my 9-5 as an HR Manager and starting my own business. Prior to our separation, I really wanted to start my own business but he was not on board.

While I was disappointed, at the time I felt like he didn't believe in me. Now this was a lie I told myself and because I did not check in back then, I was left with this belief and our marriage continued to deteriorate. I can look back now through my lens of forgiveness, grace, unconditional love, and strength and know that he loved me, he was looking out for me, it was best for me at the time, and I needed him to say no. I would have struggled and probably not have been successful. I struggled with depression and insecurities at the time, I had so much to work through. I believe God closed that door at the time to protect my heart from further damage. In the moment, sometimes it's hard for us to look at our situations as a blessing in disguise. Knowing this now, I see things much differently. When my husband says, "No" to anything, I look through the "He Loves Me" Lens. I can do this because I believe in him, I believe in us, and our marriage.

Do you check in with your heart and your spouse's heart?

Journal Time ~ Write Out Beliefs. Are you constantly withdrawing from your account (relationship) and not putting in any deposits (believing & love)? I'm sure you probably cook, clean, iron clothes, do the laundry, work long hours, care for the kids, and speak many loving/positive words to your spouse daily...right? Or maybe you're out there working hard to provide for your family, taking out the trash, making sure your doors are locked at night, etc. You do all of this because you believe in your love and therefore you want to give and live out your purpose as the best partner you can be...right? Consider your heart, how you care and love for your family, and why. Write all about it.

I use to lack in being loving and having positive words. Over time, I began to lack in cleaning up the house consistently. I would clean and within days, we had piles and mess again. I could always gauge my marriage on how messy my house was. The main reason I cleaned and played this role of wife was more based on what was just ingrained in me that was what wives did. It wasn't because I was so happy or in love, I simple operated out of what I saw or thought I was supposed to do. I never knew or understood that marriage was so much deeper and required a deeper understanding of who I was and what I believed.

We all play a role in our home, we can only take on that role if we believe in it. When we confuse our roles, we start to experience chaos, confusion, and frustration. Either spouse can be the one who works while the other stays home; I'm not speaking of those types of roles. But when women take on a masculine leadership role and men are forced into a feminine submission role, there can be an imbalance. I'm not a quiet, sit-in-the-back-seat kind of woman, but I believe God created my husband to be the leader and head of our home.

For years, I covered up my insecurities by being loud and "standing up for what I wanted for me and my kids." And I needed to get my mouth under control because my words were coming from a heart that was broken and confused and bitter. I wanted to control whatever and whoever I could because I felt out of control in my life. But my heart wasn't in the right place, and our home became chaotic.

Our marriage wasn't working well. I was unable to work, care for our kids, clean, cook, take care of finances, be a loving wife, and spiritually serve God. In a two-parent household, when one parent tries to take on all the tasks, the imbalance brings problems.

In a single-parent household, one person *does* do it all! I've been a single mom, so there are women out there that do fulfill 100% of the leadership roles! Shout out to the amazing women who can do all this with excellence. But in a marriage, you and your partner need to have balance in your roles.

## **Journal Time**
*Take out your journal or a notebook and answer some or all of these questions.*

## How balanced is your life?

How are you believing in yourself. Maybe you even think too highly of yourself or not at all. Write down ways you can transform your life through the way you believe in yourself. You may have let yourself down too many times and need to go back to forgiveness and work through the steps and believe in yourself again.

How do you believe in your spouse. Do you believe they are the one you've always wanted? Do you believe in who they are as a person or as a parent to your kids? Do you constantly challenge their decisions, words, or suggestions? Do you support them, even when you don't feel like it? How can you believe more in them or improve in this area starting today?

How do you believe in your marriage. Do you believe your marriage will work? Do you want your marriage to work? Do you want your marriage to do more than "work," do you want it to thrive on fierce love? Do you make "deposits" into your marriage? Are they enough? Do you live your calling and purpose as his wife? What can you change today to improve or eliminate any disbelief? Pick at least one thing each day you can do to believe in your marriage.

## *Check-In*

Do you believe in your spouse? If yes, what does it look, feel like, and do they know? If no, why?

What do you think needs to happen for you to believe in them? Why?

If you don't believe in your spouse, consider why. Is it your ego, a lack of forgiveness, or something else? How can you believe in your spouse?

Do you lack commitment to your spouse? Do you say you'll do something and not do it for your spouse?

How will you grow in this area?

 

Connect with your spouse. Does your spouse believe in you? If not, why not? What can your spouse do to start believing in you?

There are other important relationships in our lives. It may be a relationship with a child, a parent, a good friend. I have learned that in building relationships, it's important to nurture and care for those relationships also.

There have been times I tell my daughter I will sit and read with her before bed, then I get tired and tell her another night. While it may seem innocent and not on purpose, this breaks down my relationship with her, it breaks trust. It's critical to understand that believing in someone or something comes with being committed to that person or thing. When I don't stick to my commitment to spend time with my daughter before bed, she begins believing I don't value our time, she begins to tell herself a story based on my level of commitment to her. We do the same thing with our spouse or our boss, when they don't keep their word, when they make us second to someone or something else, we begin to believe lies or tell ourselves a story based on their decisions. We tend to lean on the negative thoughts first, rather than giving them the benefit of the doubt. While your reason or someone else's reason for not sticking to a commitment may be valid, it doesn't change the fact that we begin to doubt love when they're broken.

Do you believe in others in your life? If yes, what does it look and feel like, and do they know? If no, why? Think about your child(ren), close friends, etc.

_____
_____
_____
_____
_____
_____

Do you follow through on your commitments to them? If not, why not? _____

_____
_____
_____
_____
_____
_____

How will you grow in this area?

_____

_____

_____

_____

_____

What will you do differently? How will you hold yourself accountable? _____

_____

_____

_____

_____

_____

_____

KARI VAZQUEZ

## *I am so grateful for...*

# 7

## Take Action

*Faith without works is dead!*

Time to take action! How many times do we say:

1. "I know what I need to do," and not do it?

2. "I'm going to do_____," and not do it?

3. "I will start…tomorrow."

4. "I wasn't able to do ABC because XYZ."

Today, right now, commit to doing the things that need to be done. Make a list of decisions you have been putting off and get them done. Split the list up into 4 sections.

| Self | Spouse | Family | Others |
| --- | --- | --- | --- |

What do you need to take action on? Let your thoughts flow without holding back. It doesn't matter how small or big you think it is, whether you think it's doable or not, write it all down. Everything, even if you come up with an excuse to not write something down, add it to the list.

Once you finish the list, start with yourself and pick one thing you can do now. What's the easiest thing you can do for yourself? When you begin to get things done, this will grow your faith, your belief, and your level of commitment.

## LET'S DO THIS!

## **ACTION - Must Do List!**

| Self | Spouse | Family | Others |
|------|--------|--------|--------|
|      |        |        |        |
|      |        |        |        |
|      |        |        |        |
|      |        |        |        |
|      |        |        |        |
|      |        |        |        |
|      |        |        |        |

Something that broke down my marriage was the lack of commitment to getting things done. The reality for most people is, a slacker is not attractive. When we see someone or become that someone who talks about all the things we need to do or are going to do, but don't do them; it eventually gets old and dies. We need to believe and have faith in what we are called to do and take action. Once we have settled in our hearts what we believe, we must take action to work in favor of what we are called to do.

For me, I slacked in household duties, I slacked in homeschooling the kids, I didn't work out as much as I wanted to, I didn't care to take care of myself, I didn't talk to my husband much, my conversations were usually dry and cold. While I felt I wanted to stay married and work things out, I allowed my emotions to control me. As I allowed my emotions to control me, I became depressed, resentful, angry, defensive, and emotional. I literally allowed myself to get to a place where there were days I wanted to die. I felt like everyone around me was unhappy and I didn't want to care anymore. It wasn't until I hit my rock bottom, where I had nowhere left to go, but to pray and ask God to give me the strength to get up and take action! And it wasn't until I started doing what I knew I needed to do, along with having faith and believing that God was in control and that all things would work out, that I saw transformation begin in my life and marriage.

I was angry with my husband and didn't know how we'd work through our issues. When I decided and committed to having faith and doing what I needed to do, what my husband desired of me, started being who I was called to be, my heart started to align and balance. It may sound crazy, but for me it was simple things like holding his hand and letting go of an argument we had, praying for him during our separation, fasting and asking God for answers, and becoming vulnerable. My action also involved taking down the walls I had built. I had actions I needed to take as a mom and wife, and I needed to be consistent. Being self-aware of these things is the beginning of action, since we must be aware in order to do or be.

Whatever the action may be for you, take it, do it, be it. It doesn't matter what time it is, where you are, take steps toward your goals and believe you will reach them.

# **Lovework**

What action are you struggling with taking for yourself? Why has this been a challenge for you?

_____

_____

_____

_____

_____

What are the consequences to you not taking action? How are you negatively affected? _____

_____

_____

_____

_____

_____

What pleasure or satisfaction will you get from taking action?

_____

_____

_____

_____

How will you begin to take action for yourself? Identify 1 thing now that you will do now. Schedule it in your calendar, text yourself a reminder, and email it to someone close to you. These different touch points will help ingrain it in your brain and commit and do!

_____

_____

_____

_____

Who can hold you accountable, mentor you, or coach you to reach your goals? Why have you chosen this person? Reach out to this person now and seek out accountability. Call them, text them, or email them now.

_____

_____

_____

_____

_____


What action are you struggling to take with your spouse? Why has this been a challenge for you?

_____

_____

_____

_____

_____

What are the consequences your spouse will endure if you don't take action? How are they negatively affected?

What pleasure or satisfaction will they get from your action?

How will you begin to take action for your spouse? Identify 1 thing now that you will do now. Schedule it in your calendar, text yourself a reminder, and email it to someone close to you. These different touch points will help ingrain it in your brain and commit and do!

_____

_____

_____

_____

_____

Who can hold you accountable, mentor you, or coach you to reach your goals? Why have you chosen this person? Reach out to this person now and seek out accountability. Call them, text them, or email them now.

_____

_____

_____

_____

_____

What action are you struggling with taking for others? Why has this been a challenge for you?

What are the consequences to them for you not taking action? How are they negatively affected?

What pleasure or satisfaction will they get from your action?

How will you begin to take action for them? Identify 1 thing now that you will do now. Schedule it in your calendar, text yourself a reminder, and email it to someone close to you. These different touch points will help ingrain it in your brain and commit and do!

Who can hold you accountable, mentor you, or coach you to reach your goals? Why have you chosen this person? Reach out to this person now and seek out accountability. Call them, text them, or email them now.

_____

_____

_____

_____

_____

_____

_____

_____

_____

_____

_____

# **Check In**

How do you feel about all this action-taking?

_____

_____

_____

_____

Do you have anything holding you back from taking action? If so, is it an excuse or a good reason? An excuse is usually an invalid way to justify or keep yourself from doing something you need to do, where a reason usually has a valid thought or situation that keeps you from being able to do something you want to do.

_____

_____

_____

_____

If a good reason is holding you back from taking action, have you forgiven yourself and given yourself grace? If not, why?

_____

_____

_____

_____

_____


What routine or habit will you put in place now to taking more action? Or what routine or habit will you put in place if you need to give yourself more grace if you're doing too much?

_____

_____

_____

_____

_____

_____

# *I am so grateful for…*

Notice my last "Check In" ended with addressing grace. One of the meanings of grace is respite. Respite means to rest. I tend to lean on the side of overdoing and not having grace or enough rest. This is just as detrimental to your relationships. Constant activity is a sign of distraction and avoidance. If you are constantly active, what are you distracting yourself from? When we try to avoid something or someone, we tend to stay busy for the sake of doing something. Stop and address this, if it's you.

This is a great time to also ask yourself if you're feeling guilt. When you feel guilty, you may be trying to make up for that guilt. Forgive yourself. Have you forgiven completely? Remember I said forgiveness is a daily practice, because we are faced with situations each day that could be hurtful or offensive. I realized that when my husband mentioned something I didn't do, I felt like a failure, then I would spend hours and days, overdoing. I would stay up all night doing laundry and cleaning. It was my way of punishing me and him, he wanted some clean underwear...I'll give him clean underwear and he can sleep alone in his clean underwear. Take that! But there was a part of me that felt guilt and failure. Why should I let myself sleep? This is where grace comes in.

## Journal Time

Consider the topic of grace. Identify areas that you are doing things to be distracted or avoiding people or things. Are you avoiding yourself, you don't want to look at yourself in the mirror, or face who you have been? Are you feeling this toward your spouse or others? Why and how will you shift and move into a space of grace and back to where we started forgiveness?

**Meditation Time:** Take some time to be still, hold your own hand, or put one hand on your heart and one hand on your stomach, and breathe.

Take some time now to feel all your feelings, release the ones that that must go, hold on to the ones that serve you, let your love grow, and whatever is missing create it and find wholeness and balance.

I lived too many years believing that love was only found in the movies, it was all an act, so I just had to perform and act it out to be loved. In my journey to find true love, I have found that what I was looking for all this time was within me. I had to do the Lovework and recreate the meaning of love. I didn't have to accept everything I learned about love growing up, I could take from it what worked for me, and let go of what didn't. Now you can do the same.

***Be Blessed & May Your Love Be Restored!***

For more support on restoring love in your life visit www.recreateyourlove.com.

Let's Connect

Instagram: @karivazquezco
Facebook: @karivazquezco
Twitter: @karivazquezco